The Rodent Order

The Rodent Order

REBECCA STEFOFF

Marshall Cavendish
Benchmark
New York

Marshall Cavendish Benchmark
99 White Plains Road
Tarrytown, New York 10591
www.marshallcavendish.us
Text copyright © 2009 by Rebecca Stefoff
Illustrations copyright © 2009 by Marshall Cavendish Corporation
Illustrations by Robert Romagnoli

All Web sites were available and accurate when this book was sent to press.

Editor: Karen Ang
Publisher: Michelle Bisson
Art Director: Anahid Hamparian
Series Designer: Patrice Sheridan

Library of Congress Cataloging-in-Publication Data

Stefoff, Rebecca, date
The rodent order / by Rebecca Stefoff.
p. cm. — (Family trees)
Summary: "Explores the habitats, life cycles, and other characteristics of rodents"—Provided by publisher.
Includes bibliographical references and index.
ISBN 978-0-7614-3073-5
1. Rodents—Juvenile literature. I. Title.
QL737.R6S655 2009
599.35—dc22
2008017555

Front cover: A Eurasian red squirrel
Title page: A chipmunk
Back cover: A harvest mouse

Photo Research by Candlepants Incorporated
Cover Photo: Duncan Usher/ Foto Natura / Minden Pictures
The photographs in this book are used by permission and through the courtesy of:
Shutterstock: 3, 7, 11(top), 11(lower), 19, 33, 61, 63, 76, 77. Alamy Images: Arco Images, 6, 30, 50; Adrian Sherratt, 34(left), back cover; Bruce Coleman Inc., 35; Blickwinkel, 36, 51, 68, 70; Nick Greaves, 39; Rick & Nora Bowers, 42; John Schwieder, 46; Holger Ehlers, 54; Tom Uhlman, 60; Beren Patterson, 72; M. Krofel Wildlife, 73; Dennis Macdonald, 80; Renee Morris, 82; Ami Vitale, 83. The Image Works: Science Museum/Sspl, 9; Mary Evans Picture Library, 48; Corporation Of London / HIP, 79. AP Images: Durham University, 14; Royal Society, 25; Florida State University, Uthai Treesucon, 27; The Indianapolis Star, Rich Miller, 81. Corbis: Jonathan Blair, 18; Hans Reinhard/Zefa, 32; Tom Brakefield, 53; Anthony Bannister; Gallo Images, 58; Penni Gladstone/San Francisco Chronicle, 84; Jeffrey L. Rotman, 85. Natural History Museum, London: Michael Long, 21, 23. Conservation and Survey Division, University of Nebraska-Lincoln: 24. Photo Researchers Inc.: Christian Darkin, 28; Daniel Heuclin/NHPA, 34(right); Jim Cartier, 38; Richard R. Hansen, 41; Thomas & Pat Leeson, 49; Jany Sauvanet, 55. Minden Pictures: Konrad Wothe, 40; Kim Taylor/NPL, 43; Jim Brandenburg, 45; Tui De Roy, 57; Nick Gordon/ NPL, 65; Michael Quinton, 66; Frans Lanting, 86. Yvonne Chan: 56. Visuals Unlimited: Stan Braude, 74.

Printed in Malaysia
1 3 5 6 4 2

CONTENTS

Small and shy, the common house mouse is one of the most adaptable creatures on the planet. House mice often live in houses, barns, and other human-created environments where they can find a steady supply of food.

Classifying Life

The common house mouse may not seem very special. It's a small creature, only 6 to 7.5 inches (15 to 19 centimeters) long—and about half of that is tail. When house mice get into a kitchen and nibble the cereal, or devour the grain stored in a silo, they're pests. People who like small mammals, though, sometimes keep house mice as pets. And in medical or biological labs, mice are a vital aid to research. Most of the time, though, we don't even see house mice. They scurry around as darkness falls, trying to avoid the many creatures—from cats to coyotes—that eat mice.

But the timid little house mouse is a survivor. The species has traveled to all parts of the world, riding along as an unseen passenger in cargo caravans, ships, and even airplanes. House mice now live almost everywhere that people have gone, including cold, stormy islands off the coast of Antarctica. Some scientists think that there could be more house mice in the world than any other kind of mammal—except maybe humans.

Mammals are warm-blooded animals that nurse their young with milk from mammary glands. Mice belong to an order, or group, of mammals called rodents. There are more than 2,200 different kinds of rodents, making them the largest and most diverse order of mammals on the planet. Mice—and their larger cousins, rats—are just the beginning. Squirrels are rodents, too. So are beavers, porcupines, hamsters, guinea pigs, prairie dogs, mole rats, lemmings, and many others, including the capybara, a rodent as big as a sheep.

To understand how rodents are related to each other, and how they fit into the natural world, it helps to know something about how scientists classify living things.

THE INVENTION OF TAXONOMY

Science gives us tools for making sense of the natural world. One of the most powerful tools is classification, which means organizing things in a pattern according to their differences and similarities. Since ancient times, scientists who study living things have been developing a classification system for living things. This system is called taxonomy. Scientists use taxonomy to group together organisms that share features, setting them apart from other organisms with different features.

Taxonomy is hierarchical, which means that it is arranged in levels. The highest levels are categories that include many kinds of organisms. These large categories are divided into smaller categories, which in turn are divided into still smaller ones. The most basic category is the species, a single kind of organism.

The idea behind taxonomy is simple, but the world of living things is complex and full of surprises. Taxonomy is not a fixed pattern. It keeps changing to reflect new knowledge or ideas. Over time, scientists have developed rules for adjusting the pattern even when they disagree on the details.

One of the first taxonomists was the ancient Greek philosopher Aristotle (384-322 BCE), who investigated many branches of science, including biology. Aristotle arranged living things on a sort of ladder, or scale. At the bottom were those he considered lowest, or least developed, such as worms. Above them were things he considered higher, or more developed, such as fish, then birds, then mammals.

For centuries after Aristotle, taxonomy made little progress. People who studied nature tended to group organisms together by features that were easy to see, such as separating trees from grasses or birds from fish. However, they did not try to develop a system for classifying all life. Then, between 1682 and 1705, an English naturalist named John Ray published a plan of the living world that was designed to have a place for every species of plant and animal. Ray's system was hierarchical, with several levels of larger and smaller categories. It was the foundation of modern taxonomy.

Swedish naturalist Carolus Linnaeus (1707-1778) built on that foundation to create the taxonomic system used today. Linnaeus was chiefly interested in plants, but his system of classification included all living things. Its highest level of classification was the kingdom. To Linnaeus, everything belonged to either the plant kingdom or the animal kingdom. Each of these kingdoms was divided into a number of smaller categories called classes. Each class was divided into orders. Each order was divided into genera. Each genus (the singular form of genera) contained one or more species.

Linnaeus also developed another of Ray's ideas, a method for naming species. Before Linnaeus published his important work *System of Nature* in 1735, scientists had no recognized system for referring to plants and

A naturalist from the late eighteenth century made these drawings of a jerboa. They highlight the visible physical features, such as teeth, ears, and paws, that scientists of the time used to classify living things.

animals. Organisms were generally known by their common names, but many of them had different names in various countries. Two naturalists might call the same plant or animal by two different names—or use the same name for two different organisms.

To end the confusion, so that scholars everywhere could communicate clearly about plants and animal, Linnaeus started the practice of giving each plant or animal a two-part scientific name made up of its genus and species. These names were in Latin, the scientific language of Linnaeus's day. For example, the African porcupine's scientific name is *Hystrix cristata* (or *H. cristata* after the first time the full name is used). The genus *Hystrix* contains several species of porcupines that live in Asia, Africa, and southern Europe. The African porcupine is set apart from the other species in the genus by the second part of its name, *cristata*.

Linnaeus named hundreds of species. Other scientists quickly adopted his highly flexible system to name many more. The Linnaean system appeared at a time when European naturalists were exploring the rest of the world and finding thousands of new plants and animals. This flood of discoveries was overwhelming at times, but Linnaean taxonomy helped scientists identify and organize their finds.

TAXONOMY TODAY

Biologists still use the system of scientific naming that Linnaeus developed. Anyone who discovers a new species can choose its scientific name, which is usually in Latin, or once in a while in Greek. Other aspects of taxonomy, though, have changed since Linnaeus's time.

Over the years, as biologists learned more about the similarities and differences among living things, they added new levels to taxonomy. Eventually, an organism's full classification could include the following taxonomic levels: kingdom, subkingdom, phylum (some biologists use division instead of

In spite of many differences in size and appearance between a capybara (top) and a hamster (bottom), DNA research has confirmed that both animals—as well more than 2,200 others—belong to a single order of mammals, the rodents.

phylum for plants and fungi), subphylum, superclass, class, subclass, infraclass, order, superfamily, family, genus, species, and subspecies or variety.

Another change concerned the kinds of information that scientists use to classify organisms. The earliest naturalists used obvious physical features, such as the differences between fish and birds, to divide organisms into groups. By the time of Ray and Linnaeus, naturalists could study specimens in more detail. Aided by new tools such as the microscope, they explored the inner structures of plants and animals. For a long time after Linnaeus, classification was based mainly on details of anatomy, or physical structure, although scientists also looked at how an organism reproduced and how and where it lived.

Today, biologists can peer more deeply into an organism's inner workings than Aristotle or Linnaeus ever dreamed possible. They can look inside its individual cells and study the arrangement of DNA that makes up its genetic blueprint. Genetic information is key to modern classification because DNA is more than an organism's blueprint. DNA also reveals how closely the organism is related to other species and how long ago those species separated during the process of evolution.

In recent years, many biologists have pointed out that the Linnaean system is a patchwork of old and new ideas. It doesn't clearly reflect the latest knowledge about the evolutionary links among organisms both living and extinct. Some scientists now call for a new approach to taxonomy, one that is based entirely on evolutionary relationships. One of the most useful new approaches is called phylogenetics, the study of organisms' evolutionary histories. In this approach, scientists group together all organisms that are descended from the same ancestor. The result is branching, treelike diagrams called cladograms. These cladograms show the order in which groups of plants or animals split off from their shared ancestors.

None of the proposed new systems of classifying living things has been accepted by all scientists, but the move toward a phylogenetic approach is

Classifying the Norway Lemming

Lemmings are small rodents that live in northern North America, Europe, and Asia. There are many kinds of lemmings. Here is the scientific classification for the Norwegian lemming, *Lemmus lemmus*:

Kingdom	Animalia (animals)
Phylum	Chordata (animals with spinal cords)
Subphylum	Vertebrata (animals with spinal cords and segmented spines)
Superclass	Tetrapoda (amphibians, reptiles, birds, and mammals)
Class	Mammalia (mammals, which are tetrapods that have hair, give birth to live young, and nurse their young with milk from mammary glands)
Order	Rodentia (mammals with incisors that keep growing throughout their entire lives)
Suborder	Myomorpha (mouse-like rodents)
Superfamily	Muroidea (rats, mice, hamsters, voles, lemmings, and gerbils)
Family	Cricetidae (New World rats and mice, hamsters, voles, and lemmings)
Subfamily	Arvicolinae (voles, lemmings, muskrat)
Genus	*Lemmus* (three to five species of lemmings)
Species	*lemmus* (Norwegian lemming)

Discovered in 2004, the Cypriot mouse was a species new to science. Experts think, however, that the mouse may have lived unnoticed in its Mediterranean island habitat for thousands of years.

under way. Still, scientists continue to use the two main features of Linnaean taxonomy: the hierarchy of categories and the two-part species name. Expert may disagree about the proper term for a category, however, or about how to classify a particular plant or animal. Because scientists create and use classifications for many different purposes, there is no single "right" way to classify organisms.

Even at the highest level of classification, scientists take different approaches to taxonomy. A few of them still divide all life into two kingdoms, plants and animals. At the other extreme are scientists who divide life into thirteen or more kingdoms, possibly grouping the kingdoms into larger categories called domains or superkingdoms. Most scientists, though, use classification systems with five to seven kingdoms: plants, animals, fungi, and several kingdoms of microscopic organisms such as bacteria, amoebas, and algae.

The classification of living things is always changing, as scientists learn more about the connections among organisms. Rabbits, for example, used to be considered rodents, but now biologists place rabbits in an order of their own, called the lagomorphs. In the 1990s, some taxonomists said that guinea pigs and their closest relatives should be moved to another new order, because genetic research seemed to show that guinea pigs were descended from different ancestors than all other rodents. To determine whether guinea pigs were rodents, researchers did new tests on DNA from guinea pigs and a wide range of other rodents. After the test results were published, most scientists agreed: guinea pigs are rodents after all.

People have studied rodents for a long time, partly to learn how to protect themselves from rodent pests that carry disease and destroy food. The great majority of rodent species, however, do not bother humans. Small and quiet, they live in tunnels, trees, meadows, ponds, caves, and deserts around the world.

New rodents are still being discovered. An unknown species of mouse turned up in 2004 on the island of Cyprus in the Mediterranean Sea. It was the first new land mammal found in Europe in decades. Yet this surprising rodent, named *Mus cypriacus* (the Cypriot mouse), is not really new. Experts think it is one of just a few mammal species that have lived on the Mediterranean islands since before people came to the islands thousands of years ago. Like its relative the house mouse, the Cypriot mouse is a survivor.

Scientists classify living things in arrangements like this family tree of the animal

ANIMAL

PHYLA

CNIDARIANS

Coral

ARTHROPODS

(Animals with
external skeletons
and
jointed limbs)

MOLLUSKS

Octopus

SUB PHYLA

CLASSES

CRUSTACEANS

Lobster

ARACHNIDS

Spider

INSECTS

Butterfly

MYRIAPODS

Centipede

ORDERS

CARNIVORES

Polar Bear

SIRENIANS

Manatee

CETACEANS

Dolphin

PRIMATES

Monkey

kingdom to highlight the connections and the differences among the many forms of life.

KINGDOM

ANNELIDS

Earthworm

CHORDATES

(Animals with a dorsal nerve chord)

ECHINODERMS

Starfish

VERTEBRATES

(Animals with a backbone)

FISH

Fish

BIRDS

Penguin

MAMMALS

AMPHIBIANS

Frog

REPTILES

Snake

HERBIVORES
(5 ORDERS)

Horse

RODENTS

Squirrel

INSECTIVORES

Hedgehog

MARSUPIALS

Kangaroo

SMALL MAMMALS
(SEVERAL ORDERS)

Rabbit

A German mine called the Messel pit has yielded thousands of important fossils, including this squirrel-like rodent, *Ailuravus macrurus*. Scientists think *Ailuravus* lived about 49 million years ago, making it one of Europe's earliest known rodents.

CHAPTER ONE

Rodent Roots

What makes a rodent a rodent? Its incisors, or front teeth. Rodents have pairs of sharp, flat-topped incisors at the front of the upper and lower jaws. The word "rodent" comes from the Latin word *rodere*, which means "to gnaw," and rodents gnaw very well with their chisel-like incisors. They can gnaw through wood, plastic, and even metal wire.

A lifetime of gnawing takes powerful jaw muscles. When scientists examine rodents' skulls and jawbones, they can see where the jaw muscles were attached to the bones and how the muscles moved the jaws. Teeth, skulls, and jawbones also offer clues about the history of rodents. Using the fossilized remains of ancient animals, paleontologists—the scientists who study early and extinct forms of life—can trace the origins of rodents far into the past.

FROM THE FOSSIL RECORD

Paleontologists piece together the history of life on earth by examining fossils, but the fossil record of rodents is patchy and incomplete. The reason lies in the way fossils are made.

Fossils are created when animals are covered by sand, mud, or ash. These substances hold the remains of the creatures in place. Over long stretches of time, minerals from the surrounding earth or water leak into the remains and turn them to stone. Most fossils are bones, but traces of soft body parts, even fur or feathers, are sometimes preserved. Paleontologists know, however, that small animals are less likely to turn into fossils than large ones, because predators (who catch live prey) and scavengers (who eat dead animals) often devour little creatures whole, leaving no remains to fossilize. Still, researchers have found enough fossils of early rodents, even small ones, to give an overall view of rodent history.

The oldest known rodent fossils date from about 65 million years ago, around the time the last of the dinosaurs died out. Rodents evolved from earlier mammals, but scientists do not yet know whether rodents came into existence before or after the dinosaurs disappeared.

Paleontologists think that rodents evolved in the northern hemisphere—North America, Europe, and Asia. The most ancient rodent fossils found came to light in North America. They are the remains of creatures that looked something like modern squirrels. One of these early rodents, called *Ischyromys,* was about 2 feet (60 cm) long, with a mouse-like head and long hind legs. It was probably arboreal, meaning that it spent much of its life in trees.

Another early arboreal rodent, *Paramys,* also resembled a squirrel. Over millions of years, members of this rodent's family left fossil remains in North America, Europe, Asia, and Africa north of the Sahara Desert. *Paramys* and its close relatives eventually became extinct, but by that time—between 35 and 40 million years ago—other kinds of rodents had appeared. Some of these also became extinct, but some evolved into the ancestors of modern rodent families.

Squirrels, beavers, mice, rats, dormice, and hamsters had all come into existence by 30 million years ago. So had the caviomorphs, a group of rodent families that now includes cavies, guinea pigs, chinchillas, agoutis,

Platypittamys was a caviomorph that lived in southern South America around 30 million years ago. Based on its fossils, scientists think it probably looked like a modern rodent called a degu. The artist who drew *Platypittamys* guessed at the stripes shown here—fossils have not preserved such details.

capybaras, and more. Today caviomorphs are found in South America, but genetic studies show that they are descended from African rodents. The South American caviomorphs probably split away from the ancestral African stock between 45 and 36 million years ago.

How did the caviomorphs get from Africa to South America? There are two theories. The animals could have migrated across Asia to Siberia, then crossed to Alaska on the Bering Land Bridge, which connected the two land masses when the ocean level was lower than it is today. Later, the caviomorphs migrated into South America. The trouble with this theory is that although it would have taken a long time, the caviomorphs did not leave any fossil remains in northern Asia or North America, or establish populations there. The other theory is that caviomorphs came straight from Africa to South America, accidentally carried on logs or mats of vegetation that drifted on the ocean currents.

Squirrels also migrated from one part of the world to other regions, but scientists have been able to trace their path with fossils and DNA evidence.

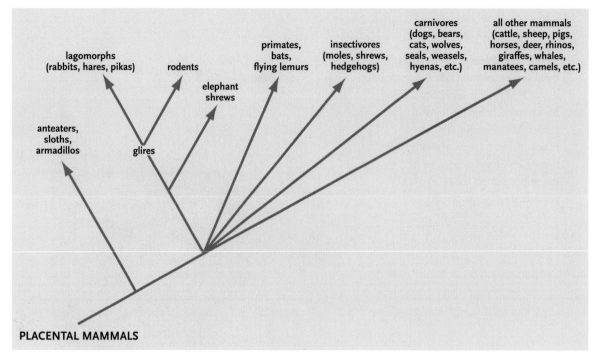

PLACENTAL MAMMALS

This cladogram shows one scientific theory about how rodents are related to other mammals. They belong to the category of placental mammals, in which unborn young are nourished through an organ called the placenta. One line of these mammals divided into two groups. One group is the elephant shrews. The other group, called glires, consists of both rodents and lagomorphs, or rabbits.

Squirrels originated in western North America around 36 million years ago. They migrated to Asia across the Bering Land Bridge, and by 30 million years ago they were established in Europe. After about 18 or 20 million years ago they made their way into Africa. Squirrels did not reach South America until 3 million years ago, when the continent became connected to North America by the land bridge known today as Panama.

HORNED GOPHERS, GIANT BEAVERS, AND TERRIBLE MICE

While squirrels were spreading through the world, other kinds of rodents were evolving as well. During the Miocene epoch, which started about 23

Epigaulus (sometimes called *Ceratogaulus*) belonged to an extinct family of gopherlike horned rodents. Both males and females of this species had horns. According to some researchers, the position of the horns suggests that *Epigaulus* used them for defense, not for digging.

million years ago, a group of rodents unlike any other lived in the Great Plains of North America. They were gophers with horns. Scientists call them mylagaulids. One species, *Epigaulus*, was about 12 inches (30 cm) long, with two short but sturdy horns on its snout. Other species had just one horn. Scientists do not know whether the animals used their horns for burrowing or for defense against predators. The mylagaulids, the only known horned rodents that have ever existed, became extinct millions of years ago.

Beavers flourished in North America and Europe during the Miocene epoch. Unlike modern beavers, which are highly aquatic and spend most of their time in or near water, early beavers were terrestrial, or land-dwelling, creatures. They probably lived in burrows before they developed the habit of damming streams and building wooden homes in lakes and ponds.

One early type of beaver called *Paleocastor* turned out to be the answer to a long-standing geological puzzle. In the 1870s, when white settlers began farming in what is now northern Nebraska, they found strange underground fossils: hollow spirals that stretched straight down as much as 9 feet (2.7 meters). People called these mysterious objects "devil's corkscrews" but could not explain them. In the 1940s, however, scientists found that the "corkscrews" had been formed between 15 and 30 million years ago by large woody vines that grew in spirals. Sand and swamp vegetation buried the vines. Later, beavers came along and dug out their centers, creating vertical burrows with ready-made walls. Inside some of the "corkscrews" scientists have found fossils of beavers that died inside their burrows.

The underground structures called "devil's corkscrews" puzzled settlers on the American plains until scientists determined that they were the fossilized remains of large, ancient vines that grew in spirals. Millions of years ago, beavers hollowed out the vines for use as burrows.

In early 2008 scientists in Uruguay announced the discovery of a 4-million-year-old fossil skull from a rodent larger than any known before. From the size of the skull (shown here next to a small modern rodent), experts think that *Josephoartigasia monesi* was the size of a full-grown bull and weighed up to 2,200 pounds (1,000 kg).

Much later, around 2 million years ago, beavers the size of black bears roamed North America. *Castoroides chicensis* was a beaver that weighed as much as 200 pounds (91 kilograms) and stood 3 feet (1 meter) tall at the shoulder. This giant beaver lived in swamps, but paleontologists have found no evidence that it built dams as modern beavers do.

Beavers weren't the only giant rodents of the prehistoric world. South America was home to a number of jumbo-sized rodents. The largest were were a family that scientists call the dinomyids. The name means "terrible mice," but the dinomyids were not mice, and they were not terrible—at least, they were probably not very fierce. They were related to modern South American rodents such as guinea pigs, capybaras, and pacaranas, and all of them were herbivores, or vegetarians.

New Family or Living Fossil?

Sometimes the best way to learn about wildlife is to see what people are eating. In 2005 scientists of the Wildlife Conservation Society visited a food market in the Southeast Asian country of Laos. Local hunters had killed forest animals and offered them for sale at the market. To their surprise, the scientists saw several small, dark-furred corpses they did not recognize. The animals had bushy tails like squirrels and long, pointed faces like rats. A look at their teeth showed that they were rodents, but the species was unknown to science.

The Laotian people called the animals *kha-nyou* and explained that they lived among rocky hills. The scientists dubbed the discovery the Laotian rock rat, *Laonastes aenigmamus*. The first part of the scientific name refers to Laos. The second part refers to the word "enigma," which means a puzzle or mystery. The Laotian rock rat was a mystery that science would not solve for more than a year.

How was the newly discovered species related to the other rodents of the world? How big was its territory? Was the rock rat rare, perhaps endangered? At first, scientists thought they had found not only a new species but a member of an entirely new mammal family. This was big news in the scientific world. It is uncommon for scientists to identify a new family in any class of organisms, but the discovery of a new mammal family is especially rare. The last time it had happened was in 1974, when the bumblebee bat was found to belong to a previously unknown family.

To compare the Laotian rock rat with other living rodents, experts carried out several sets of DNA studies. They also compared the specimens from the market with fossil remains of extinct rodents. The results showed that *Laonastes aenigmamus* did not belong to a new family after all—but the truth was just as exciting. The Laotian rock rat is what scientist call a "living fossil," a live example of something thought to be long extinct. It is a living survivor of an ancient rodent family called the Diatomydae. Until the rock rat turned up, paleontologists thought that all the Diatomydae died out 11 million years ago.

In 2006 a team led by David Redfield, a retired scientist from Florida, went looking for a live rock rat and managed to trap one. After video-taping the rodent, the researchers released it back into the wild. Redfield described the animal as friendly and furry. It looked a lot like a squirrel but waddled a bit from side to side when it walked, like a duck.

The next step for scientists will be trying to discover if the population of Laotian rock rats is large and healthy. Their research will tell whether this living fossil needs protection to keep it from becoming as extinct as the rest of its family.

In 2006 scientists captured a Laotian rock rat, a member of a family once believed to have become extinct 11 million years ago. After observing this living fossil, they released it back into the wild. Now researchers hope to study Laotian rock rats in their Southeast Asian habitats.

Before the discovery of *J. monesi,* the largest known rodent was *Phoberomys pattersoni,* which lived in the lowlands around Venezuela's rivers about 8 million years ago. It resembled the capybara, a rodent that inhabits the same region today, but was about 14 times larger.

Telicomys was one of the first dinomyids whose fossil remains were studied by scientists. At a length of almost 7 feet (more than 2 meters), it was about the size of a hippopotamus. For a long time it was considered the largest rodent that had ever lived. Then, in 2003, paleontologists working in northern Venezuela found fossils of a larger dinomyid, *Phoberomus pattersoni.* This massive rodent weighed close to a ton (900 kilograms) and measured 8 to 10 feet (2.4 to 3 meters) in body length, with a tail about half as long as its body. It gnawed its way through the Venezuelan vegetation with 6-inch (15-centimeter) incisors.

RODENTS OF THE MODERN WORLD

About 2 million years ago the world entered a period called the Pleistocene epoch. It was a time of repeated ice ages and frequent climate change. Ice sheets covered large parts of North America and northern Europe for thousands of years, then withdrew, bringing warmer weather, then formed again. During the ice ages, so much of the world's water was tied up in glaciers that ocean levels were much lower than they are today. Land bridges linked Siberia to Alaska, England to the European continent, and many Southeast Asian islands to the mainland.

All of the modern families of rodents had come into existence by 2 million years ago. During the Pleistocene, some of them experienced bursts of what scientist call speciation, which is the formation of new species. New species often form when a population becomes geographically separated into two or more groups that no longer breed with each other. As rodents migrated into new areas or adapted to new climate conditions, new species developed.

Lemmings migrated across the Bering Land Bridge from Eurasia into North America. Moving in the opposite direction, marmots (large ground-dwelling rodents sometimes called woodchucks) migrated from North America into Eurasia. Some South American rodents moved into North America. Two species of capybaras reached Florida, Texas, and South Carolina, but they eventually died out there. Short-tailed porcupines were more successful. These South American porcupines colonized North America as far north as Alaska. They survive throughout that range today.

Many new species of rats and voles emerged during the Pleistocene epoch. Two of these species would eventually become especially important from the human point of view. They were *Rattus norvegicus* and *Rattus rattus*, the Norway rat and the black rat. Scientists think that both species evolved in Asia—the Norway rat in northern China or Mongolia, the black rat in India or Southeast Asia.

For thousands of years, rats have lived in close association with people. *Rattus norvegicus,* the Norway rat or common brown rat, did not arrive in Europe and North America until the eighteenth century, but it soon became an all-too-familiar sight in cities throughout both continents.

Black rats and Norway rats are among the few rodent species that choose to live in human communities. More black and Norway rats now live in cities and other human environments than in the wild. Scientists are not sure when this association began, but it is thousands of years old. First black rats, then Norway rats moved into human settlements—villages, towns, and eventually cities. The rodents found food and shelter in garbage dumps, houses, granaries, sewers, and ships. The long and troublesome relationship between humans and rats had begun.

Paleontologists and historians have traced the spread of these two rat species along human trade and travel routes. Black rats had reached Europe by the first or second century BCE. Norway rats arrived much later, possibly not until the eighteenth century CE. Europeans carried black rats to the Americas in the sixteenth century and Norway rats two centuries later. In spite of their late start, however, Norway rats have almost entirely replaced black rats in Europe and North America. The black rat still outnumbers the Norway rat in tropical regions.

Together with house mice and squirrels, rats are the rodents most likely to be recognized by city-dwellers around the world today. The rodent order, however, contains a vast variety of other species, from flying squirrels to tunneling tuco-tucos to swimming coypus.

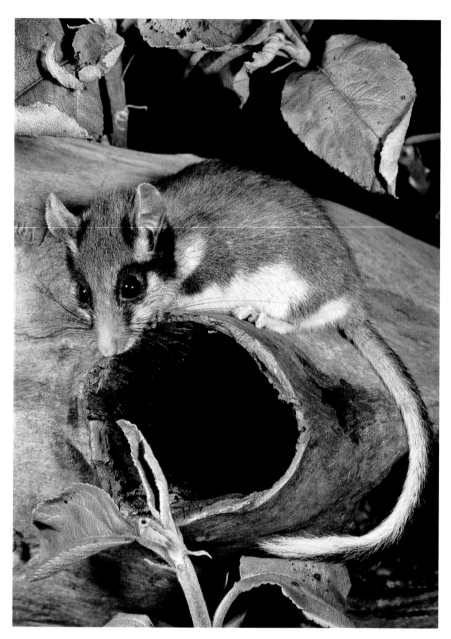

A dormouse perches on a hollow branch. Most species of dormice are arboreal, or tree-dwelling. They are also nocturnal, which means that they are active at night. By gathering the available light, the dormouse's large eyes help this rodent get around its territory during the hours of darkness.

Rats, Mice, and Many More

Rodents make up more 40 percent of all known mammal species. At least two of every five species, in other words, are rodents. More are probably waiting to be discovered in places such as Southeast Asia, the source of many of the new mammal species identified in recent years.

Scientists have different ideas about how many species, genera, and families of rodents there are in the world, and about how they are related to each other. Most experts agree, though, that there are approximately thirty-five families of rodents. They group these families into larger categories called suborders based on two things: evolutionary links discovered through DNA testing, and physical differences such as the shape of the lower jaws and the arrangement of the jaw muscles. One system of classification that many taxonomists now use divides the rodent order into five suborders.

THE MYOMORPH SUBORDER: MICE AND OTHERS

In terms of the number of species, the largest rodent suborder is Myomorpha. This suborder   contains more than half of all rodent species and about a quarter of all known mammal species. It is represented on every continent in the world.

Myomorph means "mouselike," and this suborder includes mice and rats, as well as their closest relatives. But rodents' common names can be misleading. Some species in other suborders are called mice and rats, even though they are not myomorphs, or true mice and rats. To make matters even more confusing, a few myomorph species are called dormice, even though they are not true dormice, which belong in a different suborder. (Linnaeus invented scientific naming to clear up exactly this kind of confusion.)

Most myomorphs are small. This suborder contains the smallest rodents, including the harvest mouse, *Micromys minutus*, which lives in many parts of Europe and Asia. Its body is 2 to 2.75 inches (5 to 7 cm) long,

Neither the harvest mouse (left) or Cuming's slender-tailed cloud rat (right) are endangered, but both are threatened by human activities. Modern farming aids such as mechanical harvesters and chemical pesticides destroy the harvest mouse's habitat—leading an English club to donate tennis balls for use as substitute nests. The cloud rat's habitat, the forests of the Philippines, is being logged for timber and to clear land for agriculture.

An albino Mongolian jird (sometimes called a Mongolian gerbil) blends into the winter snow. This animal's unusual white coat will be less effective as camouflage against the sand or grass of summer, however.

with a tail that is equally long. An adult harvest mouse weighs about 0.25 ounce (6 grams). The largest myomorph is *Phloeomys cumingi,* Cuming's slender-tailed cloud rat, found in the Philippines. It reaches body lengths of 19 inches (48.25 cm) and can weigh up to 4.5 pounds (2 kg).

Taxonomists divide the myomorph suborder into seven families. The largest family is the Muridae, with more than 600 species. The rodents in this family are sometimes called murids. All of them are native to the Old World: the continents of Africa, Europe, Asia, and Australia. Human activities, however, have carried some murids far beyond their native range. The house mouse and the Norway rat, for example, now live in most parts of the world.

Many kinds of Old World mice and rats belong to the murid family. So do gerbils, a group of more than 100 species that live in Africa, India, and Asia. (Some species are also known as jirds.) Native to dry habitats, gerbils

A lesser Egyptian jerboa bounds across the moonlit sands of its desert home.

and jirds have been called "desert rats," although they are not true rats. Gerbils and jirds generally live in burrows. When they come out to forage for seeds, grasses, and small insects, the coloration of their coats helps them blend into the sand, rock, or dry grass of their environments.

Another group of desert rodents, the jerboas, belong to a different family of myomorphs. Jerboas are native to Asia and northern Africa. They look like mice with large eyes, tufts of fur on the ends of their tails, and very long hind legs. Jerboas move about by walking and hopping on their hind legs. When traveling fast to escape an owl or wild cat, a jerboa can leap up to 10 feet (3 m) in a single bound and reach speeds of 7 miles per hour (11 km per hour).

The second largest family of myomorphs, the Cricetidae, has almost 600 species. Among them are the species native to North America, such as deer mice and woodrats (also called pack rats). One of the larger North American members of this family is *Ondatra zibethicus,* the muskrat, which usually weighs 4 pounds (1.8 kg) or more and has a body length of 10 to 16 inches (25 to 40 cm). Muskrats are aquatic rodents that live in ponds, streams, and marshes. They nest in holes in the bank or in piles of mud and vegetation that they create. The Cricetidae family also includes rice rats, cane rats, cotton rats, crab-eating rats, climbing rats, leaf-eared mice, Andean mice, and many other species native to Central and South America.

In addition to the New World or American rodents, the Cricetidae family contains some Old World rodents. Hamsters are plump-bodied, short-tailed rodents that range in body length from 2 to 13 inches (5 to 34 cm), depending on the species. The original range of hamsters stretched from central Europe east to Pakistan, Siberia, and northern China. Hamsters are popular pets, however, and people have carried them to most parts of the world.

Lemmings and voles are members of the Cricetidae family. These small rodents are found in North America and Eurasia. Lemmings are more limited in their range, favoring the northern regions. They are burrowers who remain active during the winter, protected by coats of thick fur, scampering along paths they dig beneath the snow. Voles have adapted to a wide variety of habitats, from forests to high-mountain meadows. The water vole, *Arvicola terrestris,* is found throughout western Europe. It is one of several aquatic vole species. The sagebrush vole, *Lemmiscus curtatus,* lives in dry brushlands in the Western United States.

The myomorph suborder includes bamboo rats, blind mole rats (eight or so species of burrowers who dig with their teeth and whose eyes are hidden beneath folds of skin), spiny dormice (which are not true dormice), and mouselike hamsters (which are not true hamsters). Zokors are also myomorphs. These fossorial, or burrowing, rodents live in Central Asia,

The Truth About Lemmings

Do rodents commit suicide? For years, people believed that a rodent called the lemming committed mass suicide every few years. Huge numbers of lemmings, it was said, marched over cliffs to drown in the sea. A 1958 nature "documentary" called *White Wilderness* spread this idea by showing lemmings leaping into the water. It is now known that the filmmakers faked that footage. They forced captured lemmings to plunge into a river and drown.

Lemmings breed very rapidly. When their numbers reach the point where local food sources—leaves, grasses, roots, and bulbs—cannot support them all, thousands of them migrate in search of new territories. If a lot of lemmings reach a cliff edge during a migration, some may be pushed over by the pressure of those behind. Lemmings can swim, and they often migrate across streams or small lakes. If the distance is too great, however, or the lemmings are undernourished, they die of exhaustion while swimming. These events gave rise to the myth of mass lemming suicide.

Greenland collared lemmings migrate in search of new food sources.

The Damaraland mole rat, native to Africa, may forage for leaves above ground but spends most of its time in an underground burrow. Mole rats, which eat worms and insects as well as leaves and roots, live together in colonies.

Siberia, and western China. Although some fossorial rodents dig with their incisors, zokors have powerful front legs equipped with sturdy claws for excavating their tunnels and underground nests.

THE CASTORIMORPH SUBORDER: BEAVERS AND OTHERS

The suborder Castorimorpha contains three families. One family is the beavers (*castorimorph* means "beaverlike"). Another family is the pocket gophers. The third family contains kangaroo rats, kangaroo mice, and pocket mice.

Beavers

Beavers are the world's second largest living rodents, after the capybaras of South America. They can be 3 feet (1 m) long and 2 feet (61 cm) tall at

Beavers, which are native to Europe and North America, are well adapted to life in the water. They are excellent swimmers, equipped with warm, waterproof fur.

the shoulder, weighing up to 60 pounds (27.25 kg). The beaver's most distinctive feature is its broad, flat, leathery tail. The beaver uses this tail like a big flipper when swimming. Other physical features also make the beaver well-adapted to an aquatic way of life. The toes on its hind feet are webbed for easier swimming. Its fur is warm and waterproof. When the beaver is underwater, it can close its nostrils and ears to keep out water, and a clear membrane protects its eyes and lets it see.

Two species of beavers survive today: European and North American. Both species feed on bark and leaves as well as on water plants. Their preferred habitat is pond. If a beaver cannot find a natural pond, it will make one by building a dam across a stream or small river. The beaver starts by working mud and stones into a foundation. It then gnaws at the trunks of small trees until the trees topple over, drags the branches and trunks to the water, and floats and nudges them into place. Once water has pooled behind the dam to form a pond, the beaver uses the same methods to build the lodge it will live and raise its young in. From the outside a beaver lodge looks like a mound of sticks rising out of the water. Inside, however, is a dry chamber. Beavers constantly maintain and repair their dams and lodges, pressing vegetation, sticks, and mud into place to block leaks. The structures may remain in use for generations.

Pocket Gophers

The three dozen or so species of pocket gophers are stocky, furry, short-tailed rodents that range from 5 to 12 inches (12 to 30 cm) in length. Found in open countryside from western Canada south to Central America, pocket gophers excavate tunnels with their large incisors and spend much of their time below ground. Some species feed on the buried roots and bulbs of plants, seldom venturing to the surface. Others come out by night to find food and to collect grass for lining their underground chambers.

This species of pocket gopher is *Thomomys monticola,* the mountain pocket gopher. It is found only in the high meadows and slopes of California's Sierra Nevada range.

The name "pocket gopher" comes from these rodents' large cheek pockets, or pouches. The animals use the pouches for carrying food back to storage chambers called larders. Pocket gophers are often called simply gophers. People sometimes use the name "gopher" for other kinds of rodents, such as burrowing ground squirrels, but only the pocket gophers are true gophers. The most common sign of their presence is mounds of freshly dug dirt on lawns or in parklands or prairies.

Kangaroo Rats, Kangaroo Mice, and Pocket Mice

Kangaroo rats, kangaroo mice, and pocket mice are a family of long-tailed rodents. Like gophers, they have cheek pockets for carrying food. All of them are New World rodents. Most live in North America, but some species of kangaroo rats and spiny pocket mice are found in Mexico and Central America. The kangaroo rats and mice have long hind legs that

Ord's kangaroo rat lives in dry grasslands from southern Canada to central Mexico. These rodents are active at night—but when the moon is full and bright they stay in their burrows, to avoid being spotted by owls and other nocturnal hunters.

give them a resemblance to kangaroos. Like jerboas, kangaroo rats and mice move by walking or hopping on their hind legs, using their tails to balance themselves. Some pocket mice, however, travel on all four legs. In dry, hot areas such as the American Southwest and northern Mexico, pocket mice may stay in their cool burrows for several months at a time during the warmest part of the year, living on food they have stored in their larders.

THE SCIUROMORPH SUBORDER: SQUIRRELS AND OTHERS

Squirrels

The suborder Sciuromorpha ("squirrel-like") has around 300 species of rodents in three families. Most of the species belong to the largest family, which contains squirrels, chipmunks, prairie dogs, and marmots. Together the animals in this family are called scuirids.

Squirrels are found in Europe, Asia, Africa, and the Americas. Some squirrel species are diurnal, meaning that they are active by day. They are also comfortable in human settings such as parks and backyards. One of the boldest and most commonly seen squirrels is a North American species called *Sciurus carolinensis,* the gray squirrel. Since being introduced into Europe, the gray squirrel has competed with smaller and less aggressive native species for food and habitat.

Gray squirrels are tree squirrels, and so are many other species of squirrels. These rodents spend a lot of time in trees, running nimbly up and down tree trunks and leaping from branch to branch, or from tree to tree. They occupy holes in tree trunks or build large round nests of sticks and leaves high in the branches. Still, tree squirrels often forage for food on the ground. Their main foods are nuts and seeds,

Another nocturnal rodent is *Glaucomys volans,* the eastern or southern flying squirrel. Native to North America east of the Mississippi River, these gilders occasionally cover distances as great as 264 feet (80 m), swerving in mid-flight to avoid tree branches and other obstacles.

although they may also eat leaves, buds, insects, or even birds' eggs from time to time.

Unlike tree squirrels, flying squirrels rarely come down out of the trees. These species of squirrels do not really fly—they glide through the air like kites. Flaps of skin run from their wrists to their ankles. When the squirrels launch themselves into the air and stretch out their legs, the flaps form "sails." The biggest flying squirrels belong to the genus *Petaurista.* Native to Taiwan and other parts of eastern Asia, these giant flying squirrels measure as much as 4 feet (1.2 m) in length, including the tail. Smaller flying squirrels are native to Europe and North America, but most people never see these nocturnal, arboreal rodents.

The tails of tree squirrels and flying squirrels are often long and bushy. Some ground squirrel species have much shorter tails. Many ground squirrels are burrowers, although they can also climb trees. Eurasian species of ground squirrels often have spotted coats. American species, including chipmunks, usually have several light and dark stripes down their backs or along their sides. Each type of coloration provides camouflage, helping the rodents disappear into backgrounds of rock or grasses.

Prairie Dogs

Prairie dogs are short-tailed, plump rodents measuring 12 to 16 inches (30 to 40 cm) in length. There are half a dozen or so species of them in the genus *Cynomys.* They are North American rodents, native to the grasslands and dry prairies of the West, although some colonies have become established in the eastern part of the continent.

No rodent is more social than the prairie dog, which lives in concentrations of burrows called towns. Prairie dog towns may cover hundreds of acres and be home to many thousands of animals. Social animals need to communicate, and prairie dogs use a wide range of sounds, including whistles and chirps when they greet each other, warning chirps, and an alarm call that sounds like the bark of a dog. Explorers Meriwether Lewis and William Clark encountered these rodents when they crossed the plains

Prairie dogs, the most social rodents, live in large colonies of interconnected burrows, and they use a variety of calls to communicate with each other. This prairie dog town is located in South Dakota. Others are found throughout the American West.

in 1802 and called them "barking squirrels." While some prairie dogs in the community forage for grasses, others stand atop the entrance mounds of their burrows, looking out for hawks, foxes, and other dangers. At the first sight of a possible predator, the lookouts sound the alarm, and the prairie dogs retreat underground. When curious, they may crouch just inside their burrows, popping up periodically to look around.

Marmots

Marmota monax, the North American rodent known as a groundhog, woodchuck, or whistlepig, is also a burrower that whistles and barks. It is, however, much more solitary than the prairie dog. Colonies tend to consist of just a few groundhogs sharing a large burrow with several entrances.

A hoary marmot surveys its territory—a rocky slope in Alaska. Hoary means "touched with frost." The name of this species refers to the distinctive white patch on the marmot's face and the silvery hairs sprinkled through its coat.

Groundhogs usually measure 17 to 26 inches (43 to 66 cm) in length, including their tails, and weigh about 10 pounds (4.5 kg), although some individuals become much larger. Groundhogs can swim and climb trees but seldom venture far from their burrows. They live in open, brushy areas in many parts of Canada and the United States. The edges of woodlands are a favored habitat.

Groundhogs belong to the group of scuirids called marmots. There are fifteen or so species in the genus *Marmota*. Except for the groundhogs, marmots are found in mountains and highlands, often burrowing among boulders in alpine rockfields. The hoary marmot, *M. caligata*, and the yellow-bellied marmot, *M. flaviventris*, live in the Rockies and other mountain ranges of western North America. Species native to Eurasia include the Tibetan snow pig, *M. himalayana*, and the Alpine marmot, *M. marmota*.

Dormice

The second family of sciuromorph rodents contains about three dozen species of dormice. These small rodents live across Europe, part of the Middle East, and Africa south of the Sahara. A few species are found in Central Asia, and one species, *Glirurus japonicus,* is native to Japan.

Dormice are forest creatures. Most are arboreal, living, feeding, and nesting in trees, although some dormice are also active on the ground. Many species of these large-eyed, shy rodents have somewhat bushy tails, like those of squirrels, and move about in trees the way squirrels do. A group called the mouse-like dormice, however, are much more similar to mice. Their short-haired tails can appear bare. Mouse-like dormice are native to eastern Europe and Turkey. They spend more time on the ground than other varieties and sometimes live in burrows. Another burrowing species is *Selvinia bekpatdalensis,* the desert dormouse, which was discovered in 1939 around Lake Balkash in Kazakhstan.

The Mountain Beaver

The third family in the sciuromorph suborder contains just one species, *Aplodontia rufa.* This North American rodent has many common names, including ground bear, giant mole, and sewellel (which comes from a Native American word). The rodent is usually called the mountain beaver, however, even though it often lives in the lowlands, and it is not a beaver.

A. rufa interests taxonomists and biologists because its skull, teeth, and jaw muscles show many small differences from those of other rodents. Experts used to think that the mountain beaver was a living fossil whose close relatives had all become extinct long age. Now, however, DNA studies have shown that the mountain beaver has ties with the squirrels. Paleontologists think that mountain beavers and squirrels evolved from the same ancestor. The two groups had separated by about 35 million years ago, but while the squirrel family has many living species today, the mountain beaver is the sole survivor in its family.

The Sleepy One

Some species of dormice *look* a lot like mice, but that's not how the dormouse got its name. The name comes from the animal's sleeping habits. Most species of dormice spend six months or more of each year hibernating. A dormouse stuffs itself with nuts, seeds, fruit, and insects during the summer, then curls up into a ball and passes the colder months in a state similar to deep sleep. Once in a while the dormouse may wake up to eat food it has stored near its nest, but it soon returns to hibernation. Even when the dormouse is not hibernating, it is active at night but sleeps through most of the day. The ancient Roman called this rodent *dormeus,* "the sleepy one." The name was used in Europe for centuries. Eventually, English-speaking people started calling the animal a dormouse. Most people thought the name came from "mouse." They had forgotten the connection with sleep.

One Englishman who knew the real meaning of the dormouse's name was the author Lewis Carroll. In his famous book *Alice's Adventures in Wonderland,* Carroll described a very odd tea party. One of the guests was the Dormouse, who kept falling asleep—until the March Hare and the Hatter rudely pinched the Dormouse and poured tea on its nose to wake it up.

Squeezed into a seat between the March Hare and the Hatter, the Dormouse dozes over its tea. Artist John Tenniel created this illustration of the tea party for the original edition of Lewis Carroll's *Alice's Adventures in Wonderland.*

A mountain beaver peers from beneath a log in Oregon's Mount Hood National Forest. This rodent is not a true beaver; it is more closely related to squirrels.

Brown and furry, with long whiskers and short tails, mountain beavers can swim if necessary, but they are not aquatic animals like true beavers. They can climb trees, but they are not arboreal animals like squirrels. Instead, mountain beavers are fossorial. They spend most of their time in their large and complex networks of underground tunnels and chambers, which they often share with other animals such as salamanders, skunks, minks, rabbits, and other rodents. The mountain beaver is unable to survive in a dry environment. It favors moist, forested habitats where it can feast on ferns. Its range is limited to the northwestern coast of the United States and the southwestern coast of Canada.

THE HYSTRICOMORPH SUBORDER: PORCUPINES AND OTHERS

The name *Hystrix* became the basis for the rodent suborder Hystricomorpha, the porcupinelike rodents. This highly diverse suborder contains some twenty families of rodents. Among them are the Old World porcupines, the Laotian rock rat, several families of African rodents, and the New World rodents known as the caviomorphs.

Porcupines

Hystrix cristata is an Old World porcupine, found throughout Europe and northern and western Africa. It has sturdy claws for digging, a rounded head topped by a crest of long fur, a blunt nose, and bristly fur. Its most distinctive feature is the long, stiff spines or quills that cover the rear part of its stocky body and its short tail. The quills on the porcupine's back may be as long as 14 inches (35 cm). To warn off predators or to defend itself, *H. cristata* raises the quills and suddenly looks much larger and more fierce. Another warning is the loud rattle made by shorter quills on the animal's stubby tail. Half a dozen other species of porcupines in the genus *Hystrix* are native to Eurasia and Africa.

If the sight of the quills on *Hystrix cristata,* the North African crested porcupine, does not scare off a potential predator, the porcupine stamps its feet and rattles the quills. If all else fails, the porcupine charges the intruder—running backward, so that the intruder gets a face full of sharp quills from the porcupine's backside. The quills can be fatal even to large predators such as lions.

Gundis, Dassie Rats, Cane Rats, and Blesmols

The African rodents of the hystricomorph suborder include several kinds of porcupines as well as gundis, Dassie and cane rats, and blesmols. Gundis are small, short-haired rodents that live in colonies, often in dry, rocky areas. The Dassie rat, *Petromus typicus,* is not a true rat. It looks something like a squirrel and lives in southwestern Africa, nesting in narrow crevices in rocky hills and outcrops. The two species of cane rats—sometimes called grasscutters—are not rats, either. Found in wetlands and well-watered grasslands and farmlands in western and central Africa, cane rats are hunted and raised for food. The greater cane rat, *Thryonomys swinderianus,* can reach lengths of 24 inches (61 cm) and weights of 15 pounds (7 kg).

Blesmols live in dry, sandy areas of Africa. There are several dozen species, some of which are called mole rats. Unlike the blind mole rats in

Two naked mole rats meet in one of their colony's tunnels. These mole rats belong to a group of African rodents called blesmols.

the myomorph suborder, mole rats in the blesmol family have functioning eyes. They are similar to blind mole rats, however, in the way they dig their burrows with their incisors. A flap of skin separates these front teeth from the rest of the mouth, so that the animals can dig without getting dirt in their mouths. Blesmols spend most of their time underground, eating foods that can be harvested from beneath the surface, such as roots, tubers, and bulbs. Some species also eat insects and worms.

One member of the blesmol family now lives in many zoos around the world. It is *Heterocephalus glaber,* the naked mole rat. This pale-skinned, almost hairless rodent forms colonies of 75 to 80 individuals in networks of narrow tunnels. Colony members often crowd together, piling on top of one another. These animals have adapted to live in conditions with poor air circulation and low oxygen. Their lungs are small, so that they can take small breaths, and their blood is highly efficient at absorbing oxygen from the air.

Caviomorphs

The New World rodents of the hystricomorph suborder are called caviomorphs. They are native to South America, although some species have migrated into Central America, the Caribbean islands, and Mexico. The northernmost member of this group is *Erethizon dorsatum,* called the North American or Canadian porcupine, which is found from Mexico to Alaska.

Some New World porcupine species are terrestrial, like the Old World porcupines. Others spend much of their time in trees. South American species in the genus *Coendou* have prehensile tails. These tree porcupines can grip branches with their tails. Porcupines eat bark, leaves, fruit, flowers, berries, grasses, and sometimes insects, worms, and small lizards or frogs. The North American porcupine is often found in forests of conifers, or evergreen trees, gnawing bark to get at the softer pulp beneath it. This species of porcupine moves easily between the ground and the trees, and it may may nest either in a burrow or up in the branches.

The Brazilian tree porcupine, *Coendou prehensilis,* has spines on its body but none on its long, flexible tail, which it uses to grasp branches. This rodent's fleshy nose is supplied with many of the special cells that detect smells, which are clues to the presence of food, enemies, or possible mates.

Cavies are a family of tailless South American rodents, including the guinea pig, *Cavia porcellus.* People in western South America domesticated the guinea pig as a food animal thousands of years ago, and it is still eaten there today. The same species has also been carried around the world as a pet. The guinea pig's closest relatives are several other species of cavies. Like guinea pigs, these are short-legged, small-eared, stocky rodents, usually brownish-yellow in color. The family also includes the maras, which have longer legs and larger ears that look somewhat rabbit-like. Native to the grasslands of southern South America, the shy, fast-running mara is sometimes called the Patagonian cavy. The larger of the two mara species can measure 32 inches (80 cm) long and weigh more than 30 pounds (13.6 kg).

Although it looks like a cross between a deer and a rabbit, the mara of central and southern Argentina is a rodent.

One of the guinea pig's closest relatives is the capybara, *Hydrochoerus hydrochaeris.* This plump, reddish brown, tailless rodent weighs about 150 pounds (68 kg) when mature. It lives in wetlands, meadows, and grasslands near lakes or rivers, feeding on grasses. When threatened, capybaras take to the water. Webbed toes make the capybara an excellent swimmer. With ears, eyes, and nostrils all positioned near the top of its large head, it can easily swim with nearly all of its body beneath the surface.

Another aquatic South American rodent is the coypu, *Myocastor coypus.* It resembles a muskrat but is at least twice as large, with adult weights of between 10 and 20 pounds (5 and 9 kg). Another key difference is that muskrats have flattened tails, but the tails of coypu are round. Like muskrats, coypu feed on water plans in marshes, ponds, and slow-moving streams. They nest in burrows in the banks. Hunted for both fur and meat, coypu have been introduced to North America and Europe, where they are called nutria.

Other South and Central American caviomorphs include pacas, which are about the size of coypu and live in forests; agoutis and acouchis, which are smaller than pacas; and the rare, tropical pacarana, *Dinomys branicki.* Sometimes called Branicki's terrible mouse, this species is the only survivor of the family that once produced the largest rodents ever known.

The pacarana is sometimes called Count Branicki's terrible rat or mouse after the Polish nobleman who wrote the first scientific description of this rodent in 1873. Pacaranas reach lengths of 31 inches (79 cm) and weights of 33 pounds (15 kg). They are the last living dinomyids, relatives of the extinct "terrible mice" of South America.

Hutias are similar to cavies but live on the islands of the Caribbean Sea. A dozen or more species are known, but about half of them have become extinct in the past eight thousand years or so. Among them was the giant hutia, which reached 200 pounds (91 kilograms) in weight.

Degus, sometimes called octodonts or rock rats, are active, alert, diurnal rodents found in the dry highlands of the Andes Mountains. They are fossorial rodents that fill their larders with food they have gathered for the winter. Their relative the cururo, *Spalacopus oyanus,* is native to the Chilean Andes. It is an excellent digger that seldom comes aboveground. The cururo finds its food underground. It eats potatoes and other tubers, as well as the bulbs of lilies.

The fifty or so species of tuco-tucos are round, short-legged fossorial rodents. They are powerful diggers that have a way of life similar to that of the North American pocket gophers. Tuco-tucos groom their fur with combs—clusters of short, stiff bristles—on their hind feet. Some researchers think that the name "tuco-tuco" refers to the clicking calls these rodents make while scurrying around in their tunnels.

Tuco-tucos use their sturdy front paws for digging and their bristled back paws for combing dirt out of their fur. The fifty or so species of these rodents are native to South America.

The spiny rats form one of the largest families of caviomorphs. These rodents are not true rats, although many of them are spiny, with coats of stiff, thick hairs. Some species are tunnelers, some live in trees, and some live on the ground, but most species live near water. In a few species, the end of the tail breaks off when a predator grabs it. This feature gives the spiny rat a chance to escape, but because the tail does not grow back, the spiny rat cannot count on using the same trick a second time.

The family Chinchillidae includes chinchillas and their close relatives the viscachas. These rodents are native to the Andes Mountains of western

A viscacha, sometimes called a mountain chinchilla, feeds on vegetation in a wetland in Lauca National Park, located in the Andes Mountains of northern Chile.

South America, where they live in colonies between 9,800 and 13,000 feet (3,000 and 4,000 meters) above sea level. Their behavior is similar to that of prairie dogs or ground squirrels. They often stand on their hind legs so that they can look around them while they eat, holding food in their front paws. In the past, wild chinchillas were hunted almost to extinction for their dense, soft, plushy fur, which was made into luxury garments—as many as six hundred chinchillas might be killed to make a single coat, using only the thickest fur from the center of the back. Today chinchillas are still bred for the fur trade, and they are also kept as pets.

THE ANOMALUROMORPH SUBORDER: TWO AFRICAN FAMILIES

Taxonomists group two families of African rodents together in the anomaluromorph suborder. One family contains a just single species, *Pedetes capensis*. This rodent is usually called the springhare, although it is not really a hare, which is a kind of rabbit. Springhares have large ears and large hind legs. They move by hopping and bounding like kangaroos, using their long, furry, black-tipped tails to balance them in midair. Fossorial and mostly nocturnal, springhares eat both plants and insects. They live in southeastern Africa.

The springhare is an African rodent that can travel by bounding on its large rear legs, covering distances of up to 6.6 feet (2 m) in a single leap and using its long, black-tipped tail for balance.

The other family of anomaluromorphs contains about nine species. The larger ones are known as scaly-tailed squirrels, while the smaller ones are sometimes called flying mice. These are neither squirrels nor mice, however. Scientists call them the anomalurids. They are gliding rodents, like the flying squirrels, with membranes between their front and back legs. Their tails are bushy or furry at the end but have bare patches covered with leathery scales near the base.

The anomalurids live in western and central Africa. The largest species in the family is Pel's scaly-tailed squirrel, *Anomalurus pelii.* It is about 18 inches (45 cm) in body length, with a tail as long as its body. These rodents have been known to glide as much as 310 feet (95 m) from one tall tree to another, although such long flights are unusual.

Scaly-tailed squirrels are as good at climbing as they are at flying. Often they simply climb from one tree to the next through the interlacing branches. Scientists think that the scaly patches on the undersides of their tails make the tails stiff enough to support the squirrels, almost like a fifth leg, when the animals are climbing—one more example of the many ways in which rodents have adapted to their habitats.

The yellow-bellied marmot, like every other rodent species, has large, straight-edged front teeth that keep growing throughout the animal's life. Rodents gnaw to keep their teeth sharp.

Biology and Behavior

Sharp, gnawing incisors define a rodent, but rodents share other features, too, both in biology and in behavior. At the same time, rodents are a highly diverse order. Their physical features and habits let them take advantage of a wide range of climates, food sources, and landscapes.

PHYSICAL FEATURES

Incisors are a distinctive part of a rodent's anatomy, or physical features. Like all teeth, the incisors are made of a somewhat soft material called dentine. On the front side, they are coated with hard, protective enamel that ranges in color from white or pale yellow to bright orange in some species. There is no enamel on the rear surface of the incisors, so the dentine there wears down as the rodent uses the teeth. This creates a sharp, chisel-like edge at the front of the incisors, making them powerful tools for gnawing, cutting, and digging.

The rodent's other teeth are molars, flat-topped grinding teeth, located far back in its jaws. There is a gap between the incisors and the molars.

RODENT TEETH

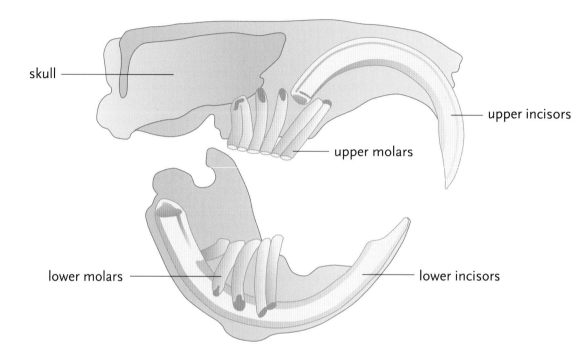

skull

upper incisors

upper molars

lower molars

lower incisors

While rodents are gnawing with their incisors, they can pull their cheeks into this gap to block unwanted material, such as dirt or grit, from getting into their mouths. Rodents sometimes gnaw on wood or other tough substances even when they are not eating, because their incisors (and also their molars, in some species) keep growing throughout their lives. The animals must use the teeth to keep them from becoming too large.

Most rodents' front paws are smaller than their hind paws, but more flexible. In many species, one toe on the front foot works almost like an opposable thumb, allowing the rodents to grasp and hold food and other objects. Species that dig a lot tend to have long, strong claws, while those that climb trees often have shorter but sharper claws that are curved to dig

A chipmunk's flexible front paws let the animal pick up and manipulate food. This rodent's natural diet consists of nuts and seeds, but bread is welcome.

into bark. Blind mole rats, which dig with their teeth and do not climb, have small, blunt claws.

Rodents' senses vary greatly from species to species, depending upon the animals' way of life. Some rodents that spend all or most of their lives underground are blind, or have weak eyesight. Those that forage for food at night, however, tend to have large eyes—the more light they can gather, the better the animals can see in dark conditions.

Nearly all rodents have keen senses of hearing and smell. Their picture of the world around them is shaped as much by sounds and scents as by what they see. Rodents rely on olfaction, or the sense of smell, to help them find food and detect dangers, such as predators or unwholesome substances. They also use scent as a form of communication.

Members of the same rodent family or colony, for example, recognize each other by smell.

Some rodents are completely herbivorous, or vegetarian. Many species, though, eat insects, birds' eggs, small animals, and—in the case of rats—human garbage in addition to plant matter. Fruits, berries, seeds, and nuts are high in nutrients and fairly easy to digest. But rodents whose diet includes a lot of grasses, leaves, stems, or bark face a digestive challenge. These foods are lower in nutrients, which means that the animals must eat large quantities to get enough nutrition. Yet the foods contain a lot of cellulose, a tough material in the walls of plant cells that is not easy to digest.

Most food is digested by enzymes, chemicals that animals produce in their digestive systems. Cellulose, though, can only be broken down with

RAT SKELETON

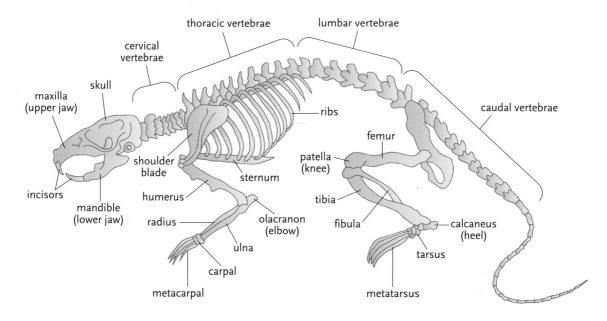

An agouti has found a piece of fallen fruit. Agoutis recognize the sound fruit makes when it falls, and they follow the sounds to find food.

the help of beneficial bacteria that live inside animals' digestive systems. Grass-eating animals have evolved several ways of using these bacteria. Cattle, deer, and some other animals, for example, have stomachs with as many as four separate chambers. As grass moves slowly through these chambers, bacteria begin to break it down. The partly digested food comes from the stomach back to the mouth so that the animal can chew it some more, breaking it down even further and releasing the nutrients. This kind of digestion is called rumination.

Rodents that eat diets high in cellulose have a different digestive process called refection. These rodents have a large chamber called a

A North American porcupine eagerly feeds on new growth during an Alaska spring.

cecum between the small intestine and the large intestine. The cecum is where the bacteria that digest the cellulose live. Food is absorbed into the body, however, through the stomach and small intestine. By the time the rodent's food is digested in the cecum, it is too late for it to be absorbed and too far down the digestive system for it to be sent back to the stomach. The food leaves the body through the anus as feces or solid waste, in the form of soft pellets that contain high amounts of water and digested cellulose. The rodent then eats these pre-digested pellets and absorbs the water and carbohydrates from the cellulose. When waste leaves the rodent's body after these materials have been absorbed, it takes the form of hard, dry feces. Only foods containing cellulose have to be re-eaten and passed through the body a second time.

The rodent order contains many small species. Being small has certain advantages. Little animals can hide from predators more easily than big ones, and they can find food and homes in places larger creatures cannot enter. Small mammals, however, face a metabolic challenge.

Metabolism is the process that turns food into energy and body heat. Animals lose body heat through their skins, and the smaller the animal, the more surface area of skin it has in relation to the volume of its body. This means that small animals lose body heat faster than large ones. The metabolisms of small creatures have to work hard to keep body temperatures

INTERNAL ORGANS OF A RAT

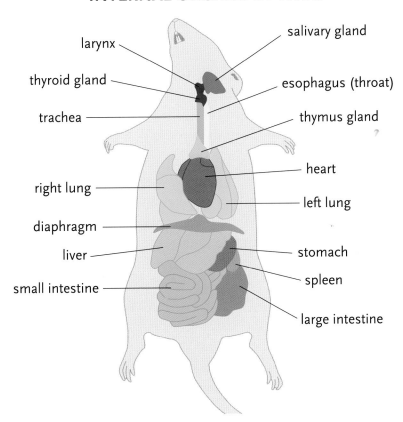

larynx

salivary gland

thyroid gland

esophagus (throat)

trachea

thymus gland

heart

right lung

left lung

diaphragm

liver

stomach

spleen

small intestine

large intestine

A hazel dormouse sleeps through the winter, hibernating in a nest of dried grass beneath fallen leaves on the forest floor. The dormouse will wake in the spring but, if food becomes scarce during the summer, it may enter torpor—a prolonged sleep similar to hibernation.

stable, which takes a lot of fuel. Small rodents such as mice, voles, hamsters, and squirrels are very active because they need to gather and eat a lot of food—some species must consume up to 70 percent of their body weight in food every day. When food is in short supply, many rodents can enter a state called torpor. Their metabolism slows down and they move very little, living on the stored fat in their bodies.

LIFE CYCLES

Most rodents have fairly short lives. Mice and voles, for example, typically live for less than a year in the wild. Dormice can live as long as five years. Squirrels usually live for three to six years, although some giant Asian squirrels have survived for up to twenty years in zoos.

Are Rodents Intelligent?

Measuring intelligence in animals—including human beings—is a tricky business. Who decides what "intelligence" means? How can it be tested? Still, for decades scientists have tested the learning abilities and problem-solving skills of laboratory rats and mice.

By studying how mice and rats learn to perform tasks (such as remembering the correct route through a maze) or solve problems (such as getting at a hard-to-reach food reward), researchers have gained many insights into how the brain works. They have also learned that, just as with humans, some rodents do better than others at learning things, remembering what they have learned, and rising to new challenges.

Rodents can seem quite cunning, especially when they avoid the traps humans set for them. In 2005, scientists released a single wild Norway rat, fitted with a radio collar, on a small rodent-free island in the Pacific nation of New Zealand. Their goal was to learn how to find and kill rats that invade rodent-free islands, before the rats can destroy native plants and animals.

Once the rat had explored the island and chosen a territory, the scientists tried various methods of trapping it. All of them failed. The scientists could not find the rat, even with the radio signal—and then, after ten weeks, the signal died. At that point the scientists found rat poop on another rodent-free island 1,300 feet (400 meters) away. DNA tests showed that it was from the same rat, which had swum from one island to the other. The scientists moved to the second island and tried to trap or kill the rat, using everything from poisoned peanut butter to rat-catching dogs. It took them two months to succeed.

Was the rat a clever, crafty creature who matched his wits against a team of scientists and outsmarted them for weeks? Humans might see it that way, but the rat was just doing what rats do: hiding, moving around a lot, and being cautious about unfamiliar places, objects, and foods.

A long-tailed chinchilla grooms her young. Captive chinchillas, which are about the size of small rabbits, have been known to live for fifteen years or even longer.

Captive or pet rodents live longer, on average, than wild ones. One of the longest-lived rodents on record was a Sumatran crested porcupine, which reached an age of more than twenty-seven years in the National Zoo in Washington, D.C. In 2002 scientists reported that a captive naked mole rat had died at the age of 28, setting a new rodent lifespan record. Although the average lifespan of wild naked mole rats is not yet known, captive individuals have extremely long lifespans for their size.

In general, small rodents generally have shorter lives than large rodents in the wild. Small rodents also tend to breed at earlier ages and to have more offspring. The common house mouse, for example, can breed when it is six weeks old. Females give birth to an average of six to eight young, although litters as large as fourteen have been recorded. Under good conditions, a female house mouse bears between five and ten litters each year. With plenty of food and no predators, a single pair of house mice could multiply to 5,000 mice in a year. A female meadow vole of the species *Microtus agrestis* can produce even more offpsring: up to seventeen litters a year, with as many as eight offspring in each litter. Mice and voles are major food items, however, for a long list of predators, from house and barn cats to foxes, owls, and weasels. Predators keep these little rodents from overrunning the world.

Baby mice and rats are sometimes called pups. Like the young of many other small rodents, pups are born in what scientists call an altricial state, which means that they are not fully developed. They are tiny, hairless, and blind, with unformed paws. Mouse and rat pups are completely dependent on their mothers for warmth, protection, and food. They mature rapidly, however. By two weeks old, house mouse pups have gained their fur and claws. They are ready to open their eyes. A month or so later they reach sexual maturity and can have pups of their own.

Some rodents, especially larger types such as porcupines, give birth to just one or two young at a time, but these baby animals are fully formed. Scientists use the term precocial to describe young animals that complete their physical development before being born. The precocial young of porcupines, for example, are born equipped with quills (softer than the quills of adult porcupines), and the young porcupines instinctively know how to raise their quills. Capybaras can walk and eat grass almost as soon as they are born. Rodents that give birth to precocial young have longer gestations—the period before birth, while the young develop inside the mother's body. A female capybara gestates her unborn young for 150 days, compared with 16 days for the Syrian hamster.

SOCIAL LIFE

Rodents are extremely varied in their interactions with others of their own species. Some are solitary. Males associate with females for breeding, and

Although these young nutria will remain with their parents for only two or three months, they will probably spend the rest of their lives in the same community. Nutria often form large, loose-knit colonies that feed peacefully together.

females raise young until they are old enough to live independently, but otherwise these rodents spend their time alone. Dormice, for example, live in individual nests and feed separately, although their feeding territories may overlap. Pocket gophers live in individual burrows and are aggressive about defending their territories from other gophers.

Small family groups are the standard social organization for some rodents, especially larger varieties. Beaver pairs often stay together for years, raising two or three young at a time. The young beavers remain with their parents for several years. By the time they set out for life on their own, the parent beavers are preparing to raise another litter. The family life of capybaras is similar, although families often join together to form herds for grazing. Being part of a herd has advantages for animals that feed in open, exposed landscapes. Although there are more mouths to be fed, there are also more eyes to remain alert for possible danger.

Many rodents, especially burrowers, are colonial. They live together in groups of varying sizes. Degus of South America, for example, are very social animals that work together to excavate and enlarge their shared burrows. They form "digging chains," lining up between the digging site and the mouth of the burrow. As the digging degus remove loose dirt, the degus in the chain pass it back to the entrance so that it can be kicked out of the burrow. Female colony-mates have been known to nurse one another's infants. Prairie dogs are probably the best-known colonial rodents in North America. Their towns can cover a large area, but they do not consist of a single huge burrow. Instead, family groups called coteries share burrows. A colony is made up of many coteries that share a large feeding territory.

A eusocial colony is one in which only one female, called the queen, bears young, while the other members of the colony feed and care for the queen and the young. Eusocial organization is typical of ants, termites, and

Cape ground squirrels, native to dry regions of southern Africa, share their burrows with several species of mongooses. Scientists think that the squirrels benefit from associating with mongooses because the mongooses kill snakes, which are frequent predators of squirrels. The mongooses benefit, too, because the squirrels dig burrows in which the mongooses can escape hot temperatures.

some kinds of bees and wasps. It is very rare in other kinds of animals. Among rodents, two African species are known to form eusocial colonies. They are the Damaraland mole rat and the naked mole rat.

Naked mole rat colonies have about seventy members on average, although as many as three hundred individuals have been counted in a few colonies. A naked mole rat queen mates with just a few of the colony's males. These pairings produce all of the pups in the colony. At the age of three or four weeks, the pups join the ranks of workers that dig tunnels, remove waste, gather food, and tend the newborn young. Because naked mole rats do not retain body heat well, colony members keep themselves and each other warm by huddling or piling together. After a mole rat has spent some time on the outer edge of the mass, the others allow it to work its way into the warmer center.

Naked mole rats depend on each other for body heat, often crowding together in squirming heaps to stay warm.

Whether they are solitary or social, rodents play a key role in the ecosystems in which they live. Rodents help trees and plants spread their seeds, either by passing the seeds in their feces or by burying them as food stores. Beaver dams and the burrows and tunnels of other rodents engineer the landscape. Beaver ponds provide habitat for plants and animals, and areas with a lot of rodent burrows have been shown to have less flooding and erosion than areas where the soil is packed hard.

Rodents also form a major link in the world's food chains. Giant South American snakes called anacondas prey on capybaras, while many species of smaller snakes enter burrows and tunnels to catch gophers, voles, and other rodents. In the Arctic, the populations of foxes and snowy owls rise and fall along with the number of lemmings available for food. Hoary marmots and yellow-bellied marmots are key prey species for bears and golden eagles throughout the mountains of western North America. One species, however, has developed a more complicated relationship with the rodent order. Over the centuries, humans have regarded rodents as everything from delicious treats to deadly pests.

The guinea pig has become a popular pet in many parts of the world. Many people keep these rodents—as well as gerbils, hamsters, and others—in special cages or glass enclosures called vivaria.

Living with Rodents

In the ruins of ancient Roman houses and cities, archaeologists have found clay pots called glissaries. These pots had a special purpose. In them the Romans raised a species of rodent called *Glis glis,* the edible dormouse. Cooked whole and covered with honey and sesame seeds, these dormice were highly prized as delicacies at Roman feasts.

The Romans did not know it, but another rodent was gnawing away at the foundations of their empire. According to many historians, one of many things that weakened the empire and contributed to its downfall was a terrible disease called bubonic plague. For a long time, modern researchers thought that this disease did not appear in Europe and the Mediterranean region until the Middle Ages. They now know, however, that the ancient Mediterranean world suffered repeated outbreaks of bubonic plague that claimed hundreds of thousands, maybe millions, of lives.

Bubonic plague is caused by a bacterium that infects black rats and Norway rats (as well as some mice and other animals). Fleas feed on the blood of infected rats and then travel to new hosts, infecting them in turn.

When the infected rats live among humans as black and Norway rats do, the fleas can travel to human hosts. The result is bubonic plague. Throughout history, most parts of the world have experienced large-scale outbreaks of this killer. In the fourteenth century, for example, the nations of Europe were swept by a plague that people called the Black Death. Historians do not agree on the total number of its victims, but in some regions the death toll was higher than 75 percent. Agriculture, trade, and social order broke down in many areas. Bubonic plague is just one of the ways rodents have influenced human history and culture.

HOW RODENTS HAVE AFFECTED PEOPLE

The people of the Middle Ages did not know that rats carried bubonic plague, but they regarded rats as unclean, food-destroying pests. As towns and cities grew, so did the populations of urban rats. Many cultures have legends about people with special ways of ridding towns of rats. One famous version concerns the Pied Piper of Hamelin, a town in Germany. The legend says that the townspeople hired a piper to lure the rats away with the music he played on his pipes. The rats followed him to a river and drowned. But when the townspeople refused to pay the piper's fee, he lured their children away instead.

Unfortunately, rats and mice will not really follow a musician out of town. Getting rid of these rodents is not so easy. For centuries people have developed traps and baits (poisoned foods) in an effort to rid their homes, barns, shops, and fields of rats and mice—or at least keep the rodent population down to bearable levels. Many rodents are suspicious of traps, however, or learn to avoid them. A rodent that sees another rodent caught or killed in a trap may refuse to approach a trap afterward, however tempting the bait.

Poison has drawbacks, too. Depending upon the chemical used, it may be a danger to humans or to other animals, such as pets or wildlife. The

"Rats or Mice to kill"

A professional ratcatcher of the seventeenth century carries a sign advertising his willingness to kill rats or mice. His methods might have included poison, traps, and trained dogs.

bait itself might not attract other animals, but predators or scavengers that might eat the poisoned rodents are at risk. Even when used safely, rodent poison has limitations, particularly against rats. These animals are suspicious of new food substances. If one rat dies after eating something, other rats will avoid that food. In addition, rats and mice breed quickly, which means that they can evolve new traits quickly. Rodents with natural resistance to pesticides survive and breed. Over the generations, the rodent population in that area evolves greater resistance, making the pesticide less and less useful.

One of the best ways to keep urban rodent populations under control is sanitation, both indoors and out. If rodents' access to food (including garbage) is limited, their numbers cannot increase dramatically. Predators also help. The relationship between humans and cats started thousands of years ago when wild cats discovered that mice and rats were especially numerous around people's farms and granaries, and people discovered that having cats around helped control the rodent population and save food. The result of this association is the domestic cat, one of the most beloved pets in the world today. Some dogs have also proven to be excellent rat-catchers. Dog breeders developed certain terrier breeds specifically for hunting and killing rats.

Beaver dams play an important ecological role in natural landscapes, creating ponds and wetlands for a variety of wildlife. When beavers build dams near human developments, however, the dams may cause floods in homes, schools, and businesses.

Rodents cause trouble for humans in a variety of ways. Beavers and other tree-gnawing rodents destroy trees, including those planted on tree farms. Ponds created by beaver dams have flooded homes and other buildings. Woodchucks may damage buildings when they create extensive burrows under the foundations. Prairie dog burrows are a hazard to livestock—horses have suffered broken legs from tripping in the holes. By far the greatest problems that rodents cause for people, however, concern food and disease.

Corn, rice, and cereal grains such as wheat are the basic foods of the human race. They are also choice foods for many species of mice and rats. Since the first prehistoric farmers discovered how to plant and harvest grain thousands of years ago, people have been waging war against the rodents who gnaw and nibble away at their grain fields,

The Pet Prairie Dog Problem

Prairie dogs are lively, social rodents. At one time they were sold as pets in the United States and elsewhere. In the early 2000s, however, officials at the U.S. Centers for Disease Control and Prevention identified some disease risks associated with pet prairie dogs.

Pet prairie dogs in Wisconsin became infected with an African disease called monkey pox after being around a pouched rat imported from Africa, and people in contact with the prairie dogs then became sick. Several wild prairie dog colonies were wiped out by bubonic plague around the same time, and captive prairie dogs in Texas were found to have tularemia, also called rabbit fever, an infectious disease that is carried from host to host by parasites such as ticks and flies. Although most prairie dog colonies and individuals are healthy, the CDC banned the trade in prairie dogs in 2003. People who already owned prairie dogs could keep them, but the animals could no longer be legally bought, traded, sold, or transported. Despite complaints from pet dealers and people who want to own prairie dogs, the CDC upheld the ban, calling it a necessary protection against zoonosis, which is the spread of disease from animals to humans.

corn patches, and rice paddies—not to mention the food they have harvested and stored.

The United Nations Food and Agriculture Organization (FAO) has estimated that between 10 and 30 percent of the food produced around the world each year is lost to insect and rodent pests. It is difficult to know how much of that damage is caused by rodents. Estimates of crop losses due to rodents vary widely. Many researchers agree, though, that rodents destroy at least $1 billion worth of food each year in the United States alone.

Bubonic plague is not the only disease spread by rodents. According to the U.S. Centers for Disease Control and Prevention, rodents spread about thirty-five diseases that affect people. Sometimes the rodents are indirect carriers of the disease. Rodent parasites such as ticks and sandflies are the

Norway rats feast on grain stored in a shed. Rodents have been a problem for farmers since the dawn of agriculture.

Scientists examine a rat trapped in Cairo, Egypt. They are studying the diseases spread by ticks, lice, and mites that live on rats and feed on their blood.

true spreaders of diseases such as typhus, which can be fatal to humans, and leishmaniasis, which produces skin ulcers. Rodents also transmit some diseases directly to humans. The droppings of deer mice, for example, contain hantaviruses, which can cause a serious and potentially fatal lung disease in people who breathe dust contaminated with dried droppings. Leptiospirosis, an infectious disease of the liver, is spread in the urine of infected rodents, which may contaminate food, water, or dust.

HOW PEOPLE HAVE AFFECTED RODENTS

A few hundred years ago, people hunted beavers for their fur and also for their scent glands, which contain a waxy substance called castoreum, used in medicines and perfumes. European beavers were wiped out throughout most of their range, and North American beavers disappeared from large parts of the continent. Then, in the nineteenth century, castoreum was found to have no real medicinal value, and the fashion for hats made out of beaver fur died away. Beavers slowly began returning to their former range. They are just one of many rodents that humans have hunted.

Chinchillas, coypus (nutria), and muskrats have been hunted in the wild and raised in captivity for their fur. Rodents have also been hunted or raised as food. Guinea pigs and capybaras in South America, cane rats in Africa, and pouched rats and other rodents in Asia are major sources of protein in people's diets. Dormice, once popular with the ancient Romans, are still eaten in parts of Europe. People in North America eat squirrels, although this is less common than it used to be.

People have found plenty of other uses for rodents, too. Mice and rats, so often the carriers of disease, are the most widely used animals for biological and medical research. Strains of disease-free mice and rats are carefully bred for laboratory use. In the late 1960s and the 1970s, lab mice had the distinction of being the first creatures on Earth to be exposed to rocks and dust brought from the Moon by astronauts. When the mice remained healthy, scientists decided that the lunar materials were free of dangerous bacteria or viruses.

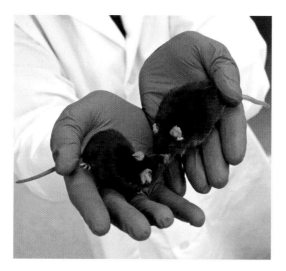

Laboratory mice are essential to biomedical research. The mouse on the right has a gene believed to be related to obesity. The mouse on the left does not have the gene and is thin. By identifying the gene, researchers may be paving the way to a drug that could treat obesity and related diseases such as diabetes.

Rodents have meant many things to different people. Hindu worshippers in northwestern India, for example, believe that rats are sacred because they will be reincarnated as holy men. People bring offerings of milk and grain to the temples for the rats.

Many rodents, especially the smaller and more social species, have proved to be pleasing pets. The practice of keeping and breeding mice and rats as pets dates back several hundred years in Europe and China. Varieties with special coloring, long fur, tufts on their ears, or other distinctive features are called fancy mice and fancy rats. Guinea pigs, hamsters, and gerbils are also popular pets. Interest is growing in less familiar rodents, such as South American degus, spiny mice, and African gundis, all of which appear to make good pets.

THE FUTURE OF RODENTS

The house mouse and the Norway rat need not worry about their futures. They are now found in nearly all parts of the world. They can live almost

At about the size of a rabbit, the giant jumping rat is the largest rodent on Madagascar, an island off the east coast of Africa. Like many of Madagascar's unique animals, the giant jumping rat is critically endangered due to habitat loss. People are clearing the island's forests at a rapid rate.

anywhere and eat almost anything. These rodents are not just hardy—they are frustratingly difficult to kill. These and other species of rodents that have large geographic ranges and high population numbers will undoubtedly survive for some time.

Rodents, however, make up a highly diverse order. Many of the world's rodent species are more fragile than the house mouse and the Norway rat. Each year the World Conservation Union (IUCN), an international association of wildlife and environmental organizations, publishes the Red List, which gives the status of as many species of plants and animals as possible. In the 2007 Red List, the IUCN reported on 2,040 species of rodents. Of those species, 315—more than 15 percent of the rodent species evaluated that year—were either critically endangered, endangered, or vulnerable (at high risk of becoming endangered). Thirty-one species, including

Darwin's Galapagos mouse and the Santa Lucia giant rice rat, were determined to be recently extinct.

Habitat loss is the biggest threat to rodents. Species that live in specialized habitats or limited geographic ranges are in the greatest danger of extinction. The history of native Caribbean rodents shows how vulnerable a species can be when it lives in the most limited range of all, an island. The Caribbean islands were once home to a number of species of hutias, rice rats, and spiny rats. When sugar planters there started to regard these native rodents as pests, they imported rat-hunting predators called mongooses. The mongooses wiped out some of the rodent species. Even species that survived had their numbers greatly reduced. People also killed off several species of large muskrat that were native to the islands—in this case, the animals were hunted to extinction as food.

Today some rodents species cling to existence as they lose their habitats to construction, forestry, or agriculture. Hutias in the mangrove swamps of Cuba, saltmarsh mice in the wetlands around the San Francisco Bay, and Armenian birch mice in the forests of southwestern central Asia are just three of the many species that face uncertain future. And without rodents, a lot of other species that depend on rodents as prey could be in trouble, too.

Some nations have enacted environmental laws to protect the endangered species, but for rodents to survive in the wild, the places where they nest, breed, and feed must also be protected. Big, popular mammals such as pandas, polar bears, and tigers receive a lot of attention from people who are concerned about the future of wildlife. The humble rodents, which make up more than two-fifths of all our mammal species, deserve a share of that attention.

adapt—To change or develop in ways that aid survival in the environment.

anatomy—The physical structure of an organism.

aquatic—Having to do with water; living in water (fresh or salt).

arboreal—Living in trees.

conservation—Action or movement aimed at protecting and preserving wildlife or its habitat.

diurnal—Active by day.

evolution—The pattern of change in life forms over time, as new species, or types of plants and animals, develop from old ones.

evolve—To change over time.

extinct—No longer existing; died out.

fossorial—Adapted to burrowing or tunneling.

genetic—Having to do with genes, material made of DNA inside the cells of living organisms. Genes carry information about inherited characteristics from parents to offspring and determine the form of each organism.

herbivore—An animal that eats plants.

mammal—Warm-blooded animal that gives birth to live young and nurses the young with milk from mammary glands.

migration—Seasonal movement, sometimes in large groups, between two territories or locations.

nocturnal—Active by night.

organism—Any living thing.

paleontology—The study of ancient life, mainly through fossils.

rodent—Mammal with incisors (upper and lower front teeth) that keep growing throughout its life.

taxonomy—The scientific system for classifying living things, grouping them in categories according to similarities and differences, and naming them.

terrestrial—Living on the ground.

warm-blooded—Producing heat inside the body by digesting food for energy (in cold-blooded animals, body temperature is determined by the temperature of the outside world).

RODENT

CLASS

ORDER

SUBORDER   Anomaluromorphs   Castorimorphs

2 families   3 families

scaly-tailed squirrels   beavers
spring hares   gophers
                         kangaroo rats

FAMILY

FAMILY TREE

MAMMALS

RODENTS

Hystricomorphs	Myomorphs	Sciuromorphs
approximately 20 families	7 families	3 families
capybaras	rats	mountain beavers
agoutis	mice	squirrels
pacas	gerbils	chipmunks
chinchillas	jerboas	dormice
porcupines	hamsters	prairie dogs
nutria	voles	marmots
cavie rats	lemmings	
guinea pigs	muskrats	
octodonts	mole rats	
	spiny dormice	

B O O K S

Goldish, Meish. *Beavers and Other Rodents.* Chicago: World Book, 2002.

Hipp, Andrew. *The Life Cycle of a Mouse.* New York: Rosen, 2002.

Morgan, Sally. *Rodents.* Natick, MA: Chrysalis, 2004.

Pascoe, Elaine. *Mice.* Detroit: Blackbirch, 2005.

W E B   S I T E S

http://animaldiversity.ummz.umich.edu/site/accounts/information/ Rodentia.html

The University of Michigan's Museum of Diversity maintains the Animal Diversity Web, including this page on rodents, with links to images and sounds.

http://www.ratbehavior.org

This page on Rat Behavior and Biology has information about rat evolution, senses, breeding, and even rat-related jokes, stories, and artworks.

http://www.ucmp.berkeley.edu/mammal/rodentia/rodentia.html

The University of California's Museum of Paleontology presents an introduction to the rodent order.

http://www.handsontheland.org/classroom/04/rats_mice.html

Rats, mice, voles, and muskrats of western North America are the subject of this kid-friendly page, which has illustrations and brief descriptions of some common species, as well as links to pages on squirrels, porcupines, prairie dogs, and beavers.

The author found these books and articles especially helpful when researching this book.

Alderton, David. *Rodents of the World.* New York: Facts On File, 1996.

Begall, Sabine, et al, editors. *Subterranean Rodents: News from Underground.* New York: Springer, 2007.

Joyce, Christoper. "A Guinea Pig the Size of a Horse." National Public Radio, September 18, 2003, online at http://www.npr.org/templates/story/story.php?storyId=1435280

Lacey, Eileen A., James L. Patton, and Guy N. Cameron. *Life Underground: The Biology of Underground Rodents.* Chicago: University of Chicago Press, 2000.

Milius, Susan. "Living Fossil: DNA Puts Rodent in Family That's Not Extinct After All." Science News, Vol. 171, No. 17, April 28, 2007, p. 260, online at http://www.sciencenews.org/articles/20070428/fob3.asp

Science Daily. "Squirrels' Evolutionary 'Family Tree' Reveals Major Influence of Climate, Geography." *Science Daily,* February 21, 2003, online at http://www.sciencedaily.com/releases/2003/02/030221080311.htm

Sterry, Paul. *Beavers and Other Rodents.* New York: Todtri, 1998.

Thorington, Jr., Richard W. and Katie Ferrell. *Squirrels: The Animal Answer Guide.* Baltimore: Johns Hopkins University Press, 2006.

Wolff, Jerry O. and Paul W. Sherman. *Rodent Societies: An Ecological and Evolutionary Perspective.* Chicago: University of Chicago Press, 2007.

I N D E X

Page numbers in **boldface** are illustrations.

A B O U T   T H E   A U T H O R

Rebecca Stefoff is the author of a number of books on scientific subjects for young readers. She has explored the world of plants and animals in Marshall Cavendish's Living Things series and in several volumes of the AnimalWays series, also published by Marshall Cavendish. For the Family Trees series, she has authored books on primates, flowering plants, and more. Stefoff has also written about evolution in *Charles Darwin and the Evolution Revolution* (Oxford University Press, 1996), and she appeared in the *A&E Biography* program on Darwin and his work. Stefoff lives in Portland, Oregon. You can learn more about her and her books at www.rebeccastefoff.com.